Canadian Sub-Urban Self-Sufficiency

M.E. Roberts-Seymour, P.Eng., OFS

========

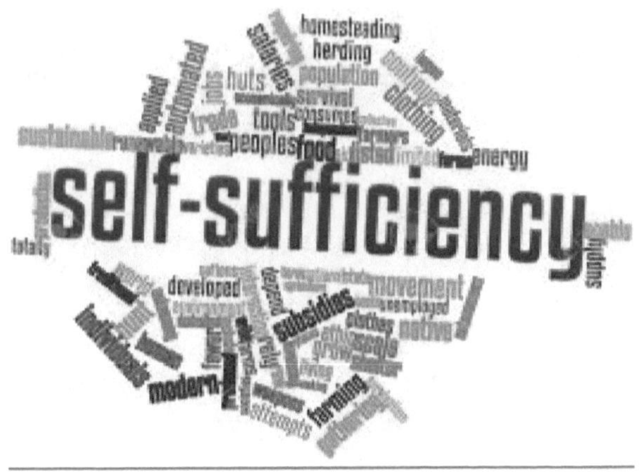

Published by Union of the Poor in Canada Press
1018 – 4900 – 20th Street
Vernon, BC, Canada, V1T 9W3

Library of Congress Cataloguing:
Mark E. Roberts-Seymour, Peng., CD (1948-)
Canadian Sub-Urban Self-Sufficiency
1. Sociology, 2. Farming, 3. Title

ISBN 9781719829519

Sub-Urban Self-Sufficiency

Table of Contents

Error! Hyperlink reference not valid.M.E. Roberts-Seymour, P.Eng., OFS 1

Introduction 43

Maslow.. 11

   The Original Hierarchy of Needs........................... 14

Hierarchy-of-Needs Summary 16

   The 'Second' Hierarchy-of-Motivation 17

   Self-actualization 19

   Recent Study... 22

"Changing" for Self-Sufficiency 25

The Nuts and Bolts of Building 43

Sub-Urban Self Sufficiency...................................... 43

   Food – Vegetables and Fruits 43

   Seeds 45

   Soil pH... 47

Animals 55

Energy 64

   Solar Capture 64

   Wind Capture 69

   Bio Diesel and Ethanol.. 74

Water 77

Selected Readings... 81

About the Author... 92

~~C~~Canadian Sub-Urban Self-Sufficiency

Mark Roberts-Seymour, PEng, CD

Introduction

This ~~article~~ <u>book</u> is directed to a readership that either; is already situated in suburban settings or are committed to realising this as a goal. The basic premises are:

- That the preponderance of Canadians have opted for suburban or ex-urban housing (circa 86%)
- That a detached house is present
- That Self Sufficiency is a goal of the reader
- That ~~Self Sufficient~~<u>Self-Sufficient</u> households can be largely achieved with 'stepped' modest amortised costs
- That Self Sufficiency begs knowledge, and therefore demands a learning curve

- That investment and re-investment in infrastructure will result in long-range economies.

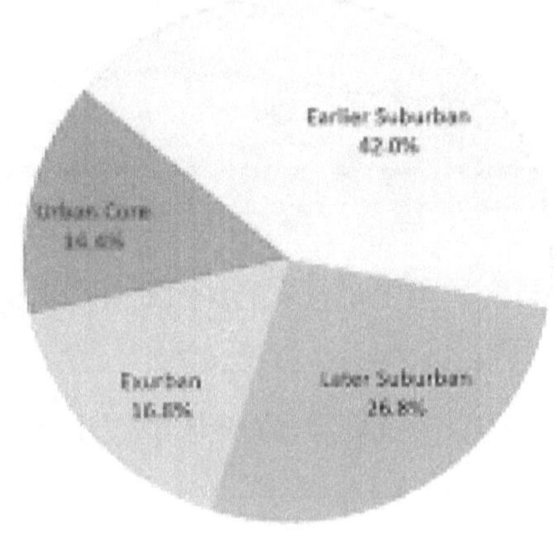

Figure 3

Canadian rural households have been static for most of the last century, though numbers have slightly increased in the most recent years of record.

All of humankind at one point was proto-self-sufficient. Eventually, individuals grouped together into cooperative communities, and specia

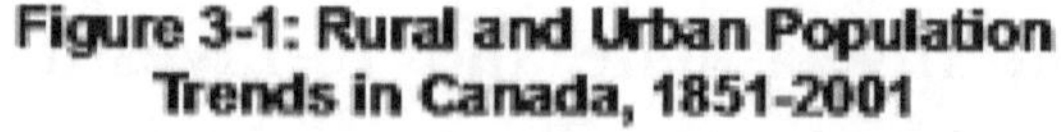

Figure 3-1: Rural and Urban Population Trends in Canada, 1851-2001

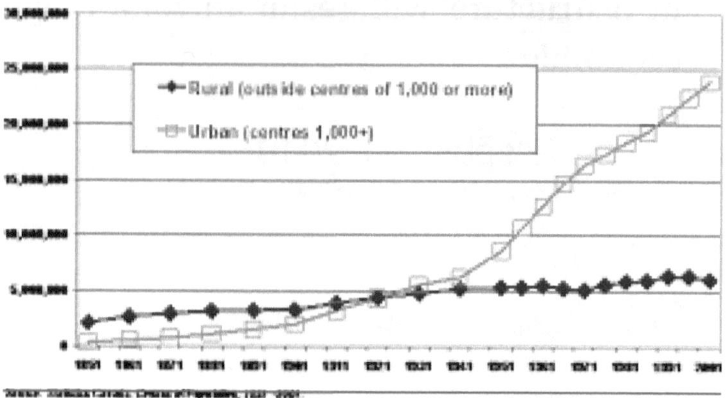

~~special~~ically<u>s</u>zation of skills and resources began to develop. Today's society is incredibly specialized and virtually all people depend on the welfare and productivity of thousands of different sources to uphold their preferred quality of life.

By regaining some measure of self sufficiency, individuals can take better control of how they use their resources and how they impact the environment. Our goal here is to reduce that reliance -- and to sharply decrease the 'costs of living'.

Complete self sufficiency may be 'unreasonable' to achieve, even if you do have abundant land, cash-on-hand, and are prepared to work yourself into an early grave.

But measured and gradually realized self sufficiency is open to anyone who is interested and has some resources behind them. How self sufficient you aim for will depend on your means, abilities and the level of comfort/lifestyle you desire.

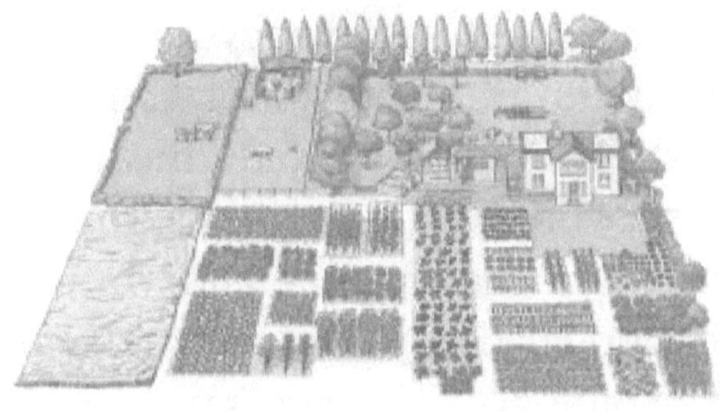

A 2.5 Hectare Sustainable Property

There are many reasons to become more self sufficient, not the least of which is the benefits it can have for the environment by reducing different types of pollution and consumption of non-renewable resources. It has been demonstrated that even small steps toward self sufficiency permit you to retain more 'cash-in your-pocket'. The four principal motivators to become self sufficient are:

1. Emergency Preparedness against natural and man-made disasters

2. Skill Development which eliminates reliance on external specialists and systems
3. Economic Advantages
4. Personal Satisfaction/Self Esteem and Peer Admiration

If you choose self sufficiency as a post-wage strategy; it is as much about reducing your outlay as maximizing your income. Every dollar that you earn, you pay tax on, and the rate varies on the country and your income, but every dollar that you save, you keep 100%. Retirees some 20 years ago saw income from savings accrue at interest rates were 18%, but now they are 5% - and they are finding that they have much less to live on. By maximizing self-reliance, you are insulating yourself from most external forces over which you have no control, including economic cycles. This however can have a dramatic effect on your lifestyle.

There are other benefits from a self-sufficient lifestyle:

- Boredom is never an issue.

- Improved health due to improved diet (if you grow your own you, eat it fresh (or preserved) and keep an eye on how it was 'raised'.)
- Improved health due to continued exercise – admittedly there will be as much or as little of his as you want, but generally gardening, cooking, power generation, working with animals etc. carried more exercise with it than crashing out in front of TV reality programmes.
- Reduced exposure (e.g. strikes, protectionist tariffs, terrorist actions, inflation, bird-flu or progressively exorbitant utility rate increases).
- Reduced environmental footprint (you are more "green").

A lot of Self sufficiency is not for the un-informed; the more you learn and retain -- the better positioned. To generate ~~power~~power, you need to be able to set up solar panels or a wind generator, manage batteries and regulate your demand so that it dos not outstrip your supply. It requires more knowledge and experience than what is required to plug in to the power grid electricity supply and flip a switch. The rewards are there; and not only monetary ones. There is also a considerable degree of satisfaction to be had by being able to provide for yourself.

The very first step in self sufficiency preparation should be to have 'Evacuation Bags'. It is a crucial backup to whatever food storage measures you use. It contains the very basics that you would want to have with you if you need to leave your home in a hurry, in backpack(s), which are easy to carry: Food (dehydrated, yielding 2000 calories per day per person), bottled water (4 litres of potable water per day per person – 28 litres per week rotated annually), shelter 'tent(s), warmth (sleeping robes) and first aid. Add one week worth of food for all concerned – and include:

1. Change of clothing based on current climate

2. Good quality first aid kit

3. Pliers, screwdrivers, can opener and glue

4. Copies of all your important documents (e.g. Wills, Insurance papers. Identification – birth certificates, social security cards and photo ID, Bank statements, Titles and deeds)

5. Cash in small bills and coins

6. List of emergency address and phone contact information, both personal and family

Do Not Raid this collection for camping trips or to supplement supplies of daily living. Keep these in dedicated and segregated back packs. Remember that water weighs one kilogram per litre – so do not make backpacks too heavy for easy carriage.

Maslow

Psychologist Abraham Maslow (1908 –1970) kept refining, over a career spanning 40 years, a hierarchy of needs and a motivational theory of psychology resulting initially (1943) in a five-tier model of human needs, often depicted as hierarchical levels within a pyramid. These needs and the subsets outlined by Maslow can form a reasonable foundation for goal setting and habit modification.

Maslow (1943, 1954) stated that people are motivated to achieve certain needs and that some needs take precedence over others. Our most basic need is for physical survival, and this will be the first thing that motivates our behaviour. Once that level is fulfilled the next level up is what motivates us, and so on.

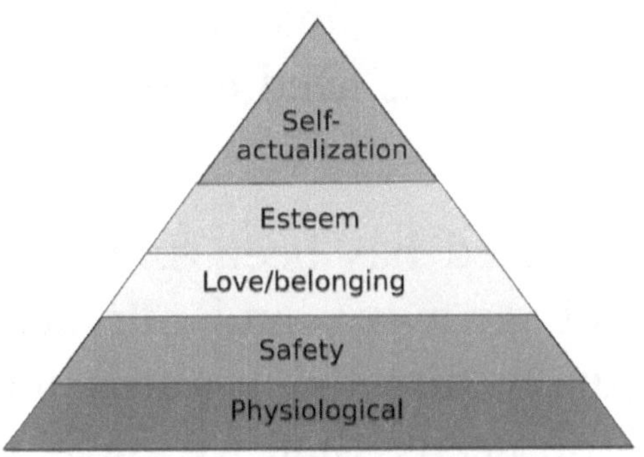

This five-stage model can be divided into deficiency needs and growth needs. The first four levels are often referred to as deficiency needs (*D-needs*), and the top level is known as growth or being needs (*B-needs*).

Deficiency needs arise due to deprivation and are said to motivate people when they are unmet. Also, the motivation to fulfill such needs will become stronger the longer the duration they are denied. For example, the longer a person goes without food, the hungrier they will become.

Maslow (1943) initially stated that individuals must satisfy lower level deficit needs before progressing on to meet higher level growth needs. However, he later clarified that satisfaction of a needs is not an "all-or-none" phenomenon, admitting that his earlier statements may have given "the false impression that a need must be satisfied 100 percent before the next need emerges" (1987, p. 69).

When a deficit need has been 'more or less' satisfied it will go away, and our activities become habitually directed towards meeting the next set of needs that we have yet to satisfy. These then become our salient needs. However, growth needs continue to be felt and may even become stronger once they have been engaged.

Growth needs do not stem from a lack of something, but rather from a desire to grow as a person. Once these growth needs have been reasonably satisfied, one may be able to reach the highest level called self-actualization.

Every person is capable and has the desire to move up the hierarchy toward a level of self-actualization. Unfortunately, progress is often disrupted by a failure to meet lower level needs. Life experiences, including divorce and loss of a job, may cause an individual to fluctuate between levels of the hierarchy. Therefore, not everyone will move through the hierarchy in a uni-directional manner but may move back and forth between the different types of needs.

The Original Hierarchy of Needs

1. *Biological and physiological needs* - air, food, drink, shelter, warmth, sex, sleep.

2. *Safety needs* - protection from elements, security, order, law, stability, freedom from fear.

3. *Love and belongingness needs* - friendship, intimacy, trust, and acceptance, receiving and giving affection and love. Affiliating, being part of a group (family, friends, work).

4. *Esteem needs* - which Maslow classified into two categories:

> (i) esteem for oneself (dignity, achievement, mastery, independence) and

> (ii) the desire for reputation or respect from others (e.g., status, prestige). Maslow indicated that the need for respect or reputation is most important for children and adolescents and precedes real self-esteem or dignity.

5. *Self-actualization needs* - realizing personal potential, self-fulfillment, seeking personal growth and peak experiences. A desire "to become everything one is capable of becoming." (Maslow, 1987, p. 64).

Maslow posited that human needs are arranged in a hierarchy: "It is quite true that man lives by bread alone — when there is no bread. But what happens to man's desires when there is plenty of bread and when his belly is chronically filled? At once other (and "higher") needs emerge and these, rather than physiological hungers, dominate the organism. And when these in turn are satisfied, again new (and still "higher") needs emerge and so on. This is what we mean by saying that the basic human needs are organized into a hierarchy of relative prepotency" *(Maslow, 1943, p. 375)*. Maslow continued to refine his theory based on the concept of a *hierarchy of needs* over several decades (Maslow, 1943, 1962, 1987).

Regarding the structure of his hierarchy, Maslow (1987) proposed that the order in the hierarchy "is not nearly as rigid" (p. 68) as he may have implied in his earlier descriptions.

Maslow noted that the order of needs might be flexible based on external circumstances or individual differences. For example, he notes that for some individuals, the need for self-esteem is more important than the need for love. For others, the need for creative fulfillment may supersede even the most basic needs.

Maslow (1987) also pointed out that most behaviour is multi-motivated and noted that "any behaviour tends to be determined by several or all of the basic needs simultaneously rather than by only one of them" (p. 71).

Hierarchy-of-Needs Summary

Maslow maintained:

(a) human beings are motivated by a hierarchy of needs.

(b) needs are organized in a hierarchy of prepotency in which more basic needs must be more or less met (rather than all or none) prior to higher needs.

(c) the order of needs is not rigid but instead may be flexible based on external circumstances or individual differences.

(d) most behaviour is multi-motivated, that is, simultaneously determined by more than one basic need.

The 'Second' Hierarchy-of-Motivation

It is important to note that Maslow's (1943, 1954) five-stage model has been expanded to include cognitive and aesthetic needs (Maslow, 1970a) and later transcendence needs (Maslow, 1970b).

Changes to the original five-stage model are highlighted and include a seven-stage model and an eight-stage model; both developed during the 1960's and 1970s.

1. *Biological and physiological needs* - air, food, drink, shelter, warmth, sex, sleep, etc.

2. *Safety needs* - protection from elements, security, order, law, stability, etc.

3. *Love and belongingness needs* - friendship, intimacy, trust, and acceptance, receiving and giving affection and love. Affiliating, being part of a group (family, friends, work).

4. *Esteem needs* - which Maslow classified into two categories: (i) esteem for oneself (dignity, achievement, mastery, independence) and (ii) the desire for reputation or respect from others (e.g., status, prestige).

5.*Cognitive needs* - knowledge and understanding, curiosity, exploration, need for meaning and predictability.

6. *Aesthetic needs* - appreciation and search for beauty, balance, form, etc.

7. *Self-actualization needs* - realizing personal potential, self-fulfillment,

seeking personal growth and peak experiences.

8. *Transcendence needs* - A person is motivated by values which transcend beyond the personal self (e.g., mystical experiences and certain experiences with nature, aesthetic experiences, sexual experiences, service to others, the pursuit of science, religious faith, etc.).

Self-actualization

Instead of focusing on psychopathology and what goes wrong with people, Maslow (1943) formulated a more positive account of human behaviour which focused on what goes right. He was interested in human potential, and how we fulfill that potential. He proffered that human motivation is based on people seeking fulfillment and change through personal growth. Self-actualized people are those who were fulfilled and doing all they were capable of.

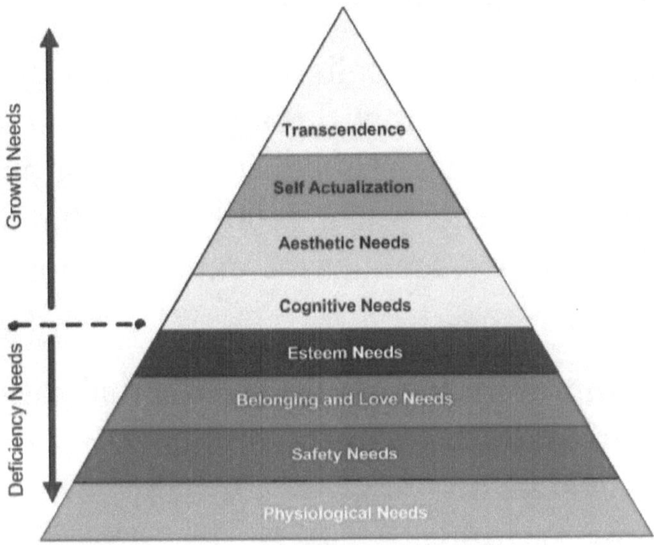

The growth of self-actualization (Maslow, 1962) refers to the need for personal growth and discovery that is present throughout a person's life. For Maslow, a person is always 'becoming' and never remains static in these terms. In self-actualization, a person comes to find a meaning to life that is important to them.

As each individual is unique, the motivation for self-actualization leads people in different directions (Kenrick et al., 2010). For some people self-actualization can be achieved through creating works of art or literature, for others through sport, in the classroom, or within a corporate setting.

Maslow (1962) believed self-actualization could be measured through the concept of peak experiences. This occurs when a person experiences the world totally for what it is, and there are feelings of euphoria, joy, and wonder.

It is important to note that self-actualization is a continual process of becoming rather than a perfect state one reaches of a 'happy ever after' (Hoffman, 1988).

Maslow offers the following description of self-actualization: "It refers to the person's desire for self-fulfillment, namely, to the tendency for him to become actualized in what he is potentially." The specific form that these needs will take will of course vary".

Instead of focusing on psychopathology and what goes wrong with people, Maslow (1943) formulated a more positive account of human behaviour which focused on what goes right. He was interested in human potential, and how we fulfill that potential.

The growth of self-actualization (Maslow, 1962) refers to the need for personal growth and discovery that is present throughout a person's life. For Maslow, a person is always 'becoming' and never remains static in these terms. In self-actualization, a person comes to find a meaning to life that is important to them.

As each individual is unique, the motivation for self-actualization leads people in different directions (Kenrick et al., 2010). For some people self-actualization can be achieved through creating works of art or literature, at home with self-sufficiency; for others through sport, in the classroom, or within a corporate setting.

Recent Study

Contemporary research by Tay & Diener (2011) has tested Maslow's theory by analyzing the data of 60,865 participants from 123 countries, representing every major region of the world. The survey was conducted from 2005 to 2010. Respondents answered questions about six needs that closely resemble those in Maslow's model: basic needs (food, shelter); safety; social needs (love, support); respect; mastery; and autonomy. They also rated their well-being across three discrete measures: life evaluation (a person's view of his or her life as a whole), positive feelings (day-to-day instances of joy or pleasure), and negative feelings (everyday experiences of sorrow, anger, or stress). The results of the study support the view that universal human needs appear to exist - irrespective of cultural diversity. The study strongly suggested that the ordering of the needs within the hierarchy is not valid as a form of 'steps'. As respects stepping through the needs from bottom to top, Denier offers: "Although the most basic needs might get the most attention when you don't have them,", "you don't need to 'fulfill' them in order to get benefits [from the others]." Even when we are hungry, for instance, we can be happy with our friends. "They're like vitamins," Diener says about how the needs work independently. "We need them all." Based on Denier's comprehensive studies we can assume working on more than one goal within the eight-layered hierarchical system is not only permissible, but advisable. Accordingly, we can begin to work on multiple levels simultaneously to realize the ultimate prize 'operating (living out) self-actualization'.

Motivational self-sufficiency is driven by all eight of Malow's ~~sceond~~second hierarchy demanding attention simultaneously – but here we are concentrating on revising conditions within the lowest two:

1. Physiologic needs
2. Safety needs

"Changing" for Self-Sufficiency

There are dozens of initial steps anyone can take to become more self sufficient. Without placing them in an order of 'timing', these should include:

1. Learn basic appliance, car, and home repair techniques (e.g. wiring, oil changing) and maintenance methods to save time and money to keep items in good repair for a longer time period. Do this on-line, in classes or ask a 'journeyman' to instruct you as he/she works on your device.
2. Use improved fireplace or wood fired space heaters to reduce heating costs.
3. Cut your own firewood from woodlots, rail easements or Crown land - and cure it at home. This requires specialized tools and vehicle use.
4. Shop selectively at thrift stores for clothes (some of which are actually

new), and for appliances and consumables at a fraction of retail costs.

5. Use indoor and outdoor clotheslines instead of a gas or electric dryer. To dry each load of washed clothes electrically requires a utility cost of approximately $Can 1.25. For a family of four this can save more than $350 annually.

6. Recycle paper products for reuse at home as scrap paper, homemade paper, packaging materials, pet bedding/litter etc.

7. Employ reusable grocery bags instead of disposable ones, and reusing store bags as trash disposal bags.

8. Growing indoor herbs and other plantings. Indoor plants have fragrance, may provide food seasoning and also transpire oxygen and humidity.

9. Opt for reusable cloth diapers that can be handed down to multiple children. A typical family can spend between $2,000 and $3,000 per baby for two years on disposable diapers while cloth diapers, accessories and cleaning with electric drying can run about $800 to $1,000. If dried by clothesline the

anticipated cost drops by approximately 70%. There is no capital outlay for succeeding children as diapers continue to be viable. If you employ a cloth diaper laundering service it will run you closer to the cost of disposables, around $2,500 to $2,800 per child-year.

10. Learn to repair, hem and sew new clothing and linens – and start doing so.

11. Learn food preservation skills such as canning, dehydration or making fruit preserves to support any harvest above immediate consumption.

12. Attend 'pick your own' farm/orchard opportunities to save on fresh produce costs.

13. Visit farmer's ~~markets .~~ markets.

14. Join food cooperatives.

15. Where required by financial constraints, make use of food-banks.

16. Choose to walk or bike instead of using a motorized vehicle. Bicycles can be fitted with large carrying capacities with basket and pannier configurations.

17. Choose energy efficient light bulbs and appliances to minimize the need for electricity.

18.   If you must have lawn, use a manual push lawn mower instead of electric or gas-powered models. Retained clippings have many uses, including rabbit feed.

19. Buy products locally to minimize the resources necessary to bring them to market and to support vendors who themselves are striving for self sufficiency. Market or barter your excess animal meat and vegetables (above household need).

20.   Start your own business to become economically self sufficient instead of relying on an employer.

21. Develop home grown beauty products in lieu of dependenceing on costly retail cosmetics, hair dye, and other products.

22.   Choose self sufficient leisure and fitness regimens such as camping, hiking, or other low impact activities that do not require extensive travel, gym costs or elaborate assistance to enjoy. They also cost less after equipment has been purchased (it has a long li- life expectancy).

23.　　Do your own maintenance about the house, and do not accumulate any clutter – especially organic waste. Tasks related to this might include basics such as painting and decorating, drilling, furniture assembly, plumbing, and so forth. Learn how to do ~~this if~~this if you don't enter a self sufficiency programme with those skills.

24.　　If you drive, do car or truck maintenance. The tasks involved may include cleaning your car, changing the oil, batteries, keeping tyres in check, and so forth. Do not purchase a new truck as part of self-sufficiency programme – a recent year used truck does not depreciate as dramatically and will serve you well.

25.　　Manage your finances in detail at least weekly. Spreadsheets which can iterate descending balances are a good tool.

26.　　Manage to incorporate a health or fitness programme into your daily life. Do chores in a manner that improves muscle, balance and flexibility. Maintaining your health is a key underpinning of remaining self sufficient — ~~and~~ and if you can make and stick to your own fitness programme rather than relying on the gym or a coach, this can be helpful.

27. Develop refined organisational skills in a variety of concurrent skills. Most often this is about making a home maintenance roster as well as external appointments and job rosters, as well as planning storage methods to save space. This is arguably the most important part of staying self sufficient and on top of everything.

28. Run a small business or businesses from your home to supplement income.

29. Ensure there is adequate lighting, water and heat for any plants you grow indoors or in a confined space. Check this before you start; if you have concerns about warmth, be aware that there are a wide variety of small plastic vinyl portable greenhouses that can be sourced on-line, in nurseries and hardware emporia, or you can make your own.

30. Make your own produce and grocery items. There are many essential items and value-added food products that you can make yourself provided you learn how and make the time. You can make your own soaps and ointments, breads, cheese, yogurt and preserves.

31. There are a lot of skill and education opportunity night or weekend classes available in most suburban communities.

32. Search the internet as a generous resource for those seeking to be self sufficient, as the many people who care about this ideal share their knowledge and information or various social media sites.

33. Also look at your local city services website to see who you can talk to in order to find out about do it yourself and self-sufficiency projects. Some municipalities have community vegetable gardens, run volunteer classes, or can direct you towards local groups who run these projects.

34. If you discover you're good at making something(s) with tools at hand,

there may be a budding business opportunity.

35.   Recycle your throwaway objects. Consider ways you can personally re-use items. For example, plastic bottles can be used to make small pots or terrariums for seedlings, while the top half can be used as a funnel. Once you start researching how to repurpose old bottles, containers, books, clothing, etc., you'll discover that the range of craft and 'do it yourself' possibilities is really extensive, giving you many opportunities for turning your old materiels into craft wares and gifts. And even if an item appears to be past its usefulness, you may be able to discover yet one more use before a final discard; for example, old clothes and towels can be used for dusting cloths or rags for cleaning. Broken crockery can be used for mosaic craft work etc...etc.

36.   Recycle things on your own (for example, making your own toilet paper from carboard): Commit to municipal recycling programmes if available, or take recycling to depots yourself.

37.	Where it's not possible or desirable to buy more equipment in order to make one craft project, or to take up storage space saving up for projects you don't have time or a commitment to make. Therefore, it's useful to connect with local craft or interest groups in your local area that would be grateful for the donation of recyclable items.

38.	Ensure that your home is stocked with adequate tools and appliances and invest in ones that you need. Source thrift stores first. Many homes lack essential maintenance tools; forcing you to throw away things that could always be repaired, or to pay for another person to do it for you. While it may not always be feasible to purchase a myriad of tools for as wide a host of 'future' needs that a large house, garden and animal support may require.

39.	It is worthwhile to obtain tools to cut wood and metal, do plumbing, maintain vehicles, modify door hinges, assemble furniture and so on.

40.	Consider purchasing (and using) an arc welder.

41. Abandoned storage facility auctions, pawn shops and thrift stores can be great places to find good tools and useful items.

42.	Invest in stocking your kitchen with durable equipment. This space is where a lot of money can be wasted if you frequently rely on consuming takeaway or frozen meals. Many modern kitchens have very little space or facilities beyond a refrigerator, sink and maybe a microwave. If funds are available, invest in a small slow cooker, a crockpot, compact or benchtop oven and a griller (And if you can, buy a food processor and a juicer (while not essential by any means, it is certainly a time saver). Other basic tools that are vital include pots and pans, decent stirring spoons, mixing bowls and small items like can openers and cheese graters; many such items can be sourced cheaply from thrift stores, online auctions and estate sales.

43.   If you can't cook or cook well, teach yourself how. Watch cooking instruction shows, make use of free online cooking schools or attend classes.

44.   If you don't have a pantry or larder, utilise other existing furniture to store food such as long-life milk, tinned foods etc..etc.

45.   Invest in a first aid kit. The most important feature of these is to effect first response to traumatic injury (viz. tourniquets, strapping, splints, gauze sponges etc.) A first aid kit is also important for treating minor home ailments, such as headaches and colds, insect bites, treating small cuts and scratches. They can also be used to store healthcare needs, such as a digital blood pressure monitor, sun-screen creams, vitamin pills and so on. And always keep a copy of the numbers of your local ambulance service, doctor and hospital in case of major injuries or health problems.

46.   Invest in a good foldable grocery cart with a liner/cover. This particularly

advantageous if you use public transit to shop.

47.   A basic survival kit is also recommended. This can be a basic box to store your first aid kit, candles and matches or a battery powered torch or lamp for a power cut, blankets and other things relevant to your needs. Many councils maintain lists of emergency supplies that a home should keep, especially if you live in an area vulnerable to such events as earthquakes, floods or wildfire.

47.

48. Get to know your local area well. The simple option is to get a map and study it and learn what businesses, community events (e.g. farmers' markets) and services are in your area. But if you walk, ride a bike or catch a local bus, train or tram service instead of driving, you can explore a lot more without having to pay attention to driving your own vehicle. Being able to walk around and know your area gives you confidence and bolsters your independence; this is helpful when you

need to find your way around your local area and ensures that you can give directions to other people too.

49.   Build a pond and raise fish for food

50.   Build an algae pond for bio-mass harvesting.

51. Freeze food as one preservation method (particularly if wild meat is a staple).

52.   Make sausage from lower grade cuts of meat. Consider hunting/trapping for meat.

53.   Explore your surroundings which may reveal interesting gems of places to see and in which to spend time. Walking around your neighbourhood and learning more about it is a fascinating way to occupy yourself if you're ever feeling bored, and is something healthier to do than watch TV or play computer games.

54.   Keep a roster of household "to dos". This might be on your computer, in a diary or on a white-board. This way you won't miss appointments or allow yourself to be double-booked. Of course, routines should be flexible, to allow you

to take advantage of opportunities as they arise. Do not be overwhelmed with attempting to do 'everything immediately'. Moreover, always look for ways to get more out of each trip you make from home, such as when going to the store to buy groceries, what other things can you do while there? Keep a list of things needing to be done in specific locations so that when you plan to go to that location, you can check off each to-do while there. Quite often it is wise to group together with family or friends to do a combined trip to save time and money. Doing this can make the experience far more enjoyable, as it also serves as a way to spend time with family and friends.

55.   Maintain a regimen to protect your mental and physical health. Physically, stay as active as possible and eat healthily. Instead of slouching the evening away, get up and walk around the neighbourhood or throw ball with your kids. Use chores as a form of physical exercise; this can make the work seem less a chore and more like

self-care. Your mental health includes teaching yourself to dispel negative attitudes/habits; remind yourself of what is good and what matters in life whenever the bad conditions cause rumination. Keep your brain challenged––learn something (anything?), do word and number puzzles, play complex games, talk a lot with other people and read widely. The portions of the brain used for problem solving are a "Use them or lose them" thing so its best to exercise the mind often in order for it to stay healthy and dynamic.

56.   Relax often. Let your body and mind recuperate through relaxation and concentration exercises such as meditation.

57.   Socialising often or talking to people helps you to remain independent. This is as important for people in married or long-term relationships as it is for people living alone––we all need a wide group of friends and acquaintances to be able to bounce our thoughts and ideas off.

58.   As we age or become sedentary, the muscle groups become weaker and the bones become less dense; this can lead to osteoporosis and mobility problems, as well as potentially reducing metabolism and undermining the immune system.

59.   See your doctor or health care provider whenever you have a need, but also to find ways to be more self-sufficient in improving your health. Use on-line resources to understand physical and mental health maintenance better.

60.   Consider and re-visit your motivations for self sufficiency and how you interact with others. Often, people want to be self sufficient due to self-perceived problems related to interacting with others, or when they simply cannot rely on others and/or look for a way to avoid people. There is a wide range of reasons people choose to be self sufficient aside from reducing waste and being more responsible as a human being. And sometimes less-altruistic or ~~inward looking~~inward-looking motivations can create other

problems which may ultimately prevent a person being truly self sufficient. You can generally gauge your own willingness to reach out and stay connected with your community by how often or willing you are to ask for help when you need it. If you stay insular from other people you create a 'difficult life'; try your best to find a way through any such alienating motivation, such as talking to others, reaching out to community mental health services or even seeking therapy.

61. Always consider novel ways to be self sufficient within your means and space. Consider advances in technologies to facilitate improvements on already instituted self sufficiency systems. The motivation towards self sufficiency comes from within. It determines how you live with what you have. Some of the best ideas come from simple needs. By looking at your local area you and seeing gaps in self sufficiency, you can improve, which in turn helps to improve your locale's sufficiency in reducing waste. And by being less dependent on outside

services, your reduced dependency can go towards those services better serving people in greater need.

62.   Try scavenging locally from untended fruit trees, and from road or rail-line berries. Make jams, chutneys or jellies from these (making certain you are not on attended property). Many edible plants grow wild (e.g. asparagus, rhubarb etc.)

63.   Source barter organisations trading skill for skill or materiels.

64.   Hunt with snares, firearms or bow for meat. Go fishing in local streams, rivers and lakes for fresh-water fish – or for salt-water fish on the seashore if it is accessible.

The Nuts and Bolts of Building

Sub-Uurban Self Sufficiency

When you start looking at being self sufficient you start consideration of the basics like food, water and energy There are plenty of other tracts that sharpen skills maximize income. Here the focus will be on minimising outlay.

Food – Vegetables and Fruits

This is one of those unavoidable expenses, we all have to eat! But growing your own veggies is not just about saving money - it is about taste, convenience, nutrients and reducing your environmental footprint. Your veggie garden can be as big or as small as you want, or are able to cope with and two tomato plants in containers on a balcony are better than nothing!

There are many ways of growing your own produce and perhaps the simplest is digging up part of your lawn and planting seeds or seedlings – if you have real property on which to do this. If your soil is not what it could be, you can make raised beds by importing organic materials such as manure, straw, hay, compost etc and or good soil and then digging it into your garden, some edging material to build up the bed and there you have it. Raised beds are a bit easier to work, and vegetables love the rich loose soil, so draining is not a problem. Begin by quantifying how good or bad existing soil is for 'agriculture'; simply adding small quantities of fresh water beach sand may improve ~~permeabilty~~permeability dramatically – provided you mix it in properly. Planting fruit trees for a personal orchard or selecting a house with mature fruit trees should be considered. If starting from scratch, choose trees that mature to fruiting quickly.

You may have difficulty with digging or poor soil so another easy way is to plant a no dig garden. This is based on making up a bed with compostables such as hay and straw and then planting your seeds or seedlings directly into it – as the bed rots down, lots of nutrients are released. Most of these constituents have to be bought though some are available for ~~free~~ - free - if you haul them away, and if your soil is poor it could be worthwhile. Use rain collection for garden irrigation. Use home-made compost and free manure to enrich your garden's soil.

Seeds

Indoor sowings or using a heated propagator can give plants a good start and ensure an even germination. Plants can go through what's known as planting 'check' when they seem to struggle not long after re-planting. Most will bounce back but it is a good idea to harden off seedlings before planting them out. To harden off a seedling, put it outside during the day and bring it in at night for around 2 weeks before planting in its final position. Alternatively start plants off in a home made cold frame, opening the frame in the day and closing the top at night. Protect seeds directly planted outside from becoming bird and rodent 'free meals'. Avoid compacted soil seed sowing, particularly for carrots, beets ~~etc..~~etc. a rule of thumb a seed should be planted no more than two to three times its size. Some smaller seeds won't need covering at all but a dusting of soil or compost sometimes helps.

A surprising number of vegetables and feeds grow well in containers. A container garden can also be very attractive is you get a bit creative with your containers, drainage is assured, and you can take advantage of companion planting. They do need the watering on hot days and, again, everything need to be bought in although recycling things into growing containers is good for the environment too. Saving seeds from the previous year's harvest to grow next year's garden is advisable. Recycle leaves and grass clippings as mulch or part of compost. Build a greenhouse to extend your growing season.

To get the maximum out of a small space, there is always hydroponics – growing your veggies in a water solution of tailored nutrient. These can be simple or complicated, such as the set ups used to grow certain "recreational" drugs. There are on-line resources that tell you how to make up your own formulae, but most people seem to buy them from hydroponic suppliers. For a small area, if you have the interest, hydroponics may work.

Whatever way you choose to grow, organic gardening (fertilizer and pesticide free) makes the most sense. Not just because it is the most environmentally friendly and gives you residue free food but because if you are going towards self sufficiency you don't want to be forced into buying expensive chemicals. Some other concepts worth study include are permaculture, crop rotation, green manure, mulching and composting.
Measure the alkalinity and acidity of soils you will use (pH balance)

Soil pH

Moderately Alkaline soils see the following vegetables and fruits thrive:

1. Artichoke (6.5-7.5)
2.

2. Arugula (6.5-7.5)
3. Asparagus (6.0-8.0)
4. Bean, pole (6.0-7.5)
5. Bean, lima (6.0-7.0)
6. Beet (6.0-7.5)
7. Broccoli (6.0-7.0)
8. Broccoli rabe (6.5-7.5)
9. Brussels sprouts (6.0-7.5)
10. Cabbage (6.0-7.5)
11. Cantaloupe (6.0-7.5)
12. Cauliflower (6.0-7.5)
13. Celery (6.0-7.0)
14. Chinese cabbage (6.0-7.5)
15. Celeriac (6.0-7.0)
16. Celery (6.0-7.0)
17. Chinese cabbage (6.0-7.5)
18. Chive (6.0-7.0)
19. Cilantro (6.0-6.7)
20. Claytonia (6.5-7.0)
21. Collard (6.5-7.5)
22. Cress (6.0-7.0)
23. Endive/escarole (6.0-7.0)
24. Fennel (6.0-6.7)
25. Gourd (6.5-7.5)
26. Horseradish (6.0-7.0)
27. Jerusalem Artichoke/Sunchoke (6.7-7.0)

28.   Kale (6.0-7.5)
29.   Kohlrabi (6.0-7.5)
30.   Leek (6.0-8.0)
31.   Lettuce (6.0-7.0)
32.   Marjoram (6.0-8.0)
33.   Mizuna (6.5-7.0)
34.   Mustard (6.0-7.5)
35.   Okra (6.0-7.5)
36.   Onion (6.0-7.0)
37.   Oregano (6.0-7.0)
38.   Pak choi (6.5-7.0)
39.   Parsnip (5.5-7.5)
40.   Pea (6.0-7.5)
41.   Radicchio (6.0-6.7)
42.   Radish (6.0-7.0)
43.   Rhubarb (6.5-7.0)
44.   Sage (6.0-6.7)
45.   Salsify (6.0-7.5)
46.   Spinach (6.0-7.5)
47.   Squash, summer (6.0-7.0)
48.   Sunflower (6.0-7.5)
49.   Sunflower (6.0-7.5)
50.   Swiss chard (6.0-7.5)
51.   Tarragon (6.0-7.5)
52.   Tomatillo (6.7-7.3)
53.   Watermelon (6.0-7.0)

Plants which may struggle in lime but do well in acid soil include

1. Blackberry (5.0-6.0)
2. Blueberry (4.5-5.0)
3. Cranberry (4.0-5.5)
4. Parsley (5.0-7.0)
5. Peanut (5.0-7.5)
6. Potato (4.5-6.0)
7. Raspberry (5.5-6.5)
8. Sweet potato (5.5-6.0

Neutral soil to modestly acidic soil preferences include:

1. Basil (5.5-6.5)
2. Carrot (5.5-7.0)
3. Cauliflower (5.5-7.5)
4. Chervil (6.0-6.7)
5. Corn (5.5-7.5.)
6. Cucumber (5.5-7.0)
7. Dill (5.5-6.5)
8. Eggplant (5.5-6.5)
9. Garlic (5.5-7.5)
10. Melon (5.5-6.5)
11. Parsley (5.0-7.0)
12. Pepper (5.5-7.0)

13.   Pumpkin (6.0-6.5)
14.   Radicchio (6.0-6.7)
15.   Radish (6.0-7.0)
16.   Rhubarb (5.5-7.0)
17.   Sorrel (5.5-6.0)
18.   Squash, winter (5.5-7.0)
19.   Sweet potato (5.5-6.0)
20.   Tomato (5.5-7.5)
21.   Turnip (5.5-7.0)
22.   Strawberry (pH 5.0-7.5)
23.   Cauliflower (5.5-7.5)
24.   Corn (5.5-7.5)
25.   Cucumber (5.5-7.0)
26.   Dill (5.5-6.7)
27.   Endive/Escarole (5.8-7.0)
28.   Garlic (5.5-7.5)

Remember to obtain seeds from mature plants for the next year's planting and thereby keep seed costs to a minimum.

Victory gardens, also called war gardens or food gardens for defense, were vegetable, fruit, and herb gardens planted at private residences and public parks in the United States, United Kingdom, Canada, Australia and Germany during both World Wars.

George Washington Carver wrote an agricultural tract and promoted the idea of what he called a "Victory Garden". They were to reduce pressure on the public food supply. Besides indirectly aiding the war effort, these gardens were also considered a civil "morale booster" in that gardeners could feel empowered by their contribution of labour and rewarded by the produce grown. The US 5 million garden single season campaign (1917-1918) promoted the cultivation of available private and public lands, realised foodstuff production exceeding \$US 1.2 billion by the end of that war. Since the turn of the 21st century, interest in victory gardens has grown. A campaign promoting such gardens has sprung up in the form of new victory gardens in public spaces, victory garden websites and blogs, as well as petitions to renew a national campaign for the victory garden. In March 2009, First Lady Michelle Obama planted a 100 m² "Kitchen Garden" on the White House lawn, the first since Eleanor Roosevelt's. Their layout, harvesting schedules and density of agriculture can be replicated and modified to suit modern self sufficiency efforts.

Buy only vegetables and fruits seeds and bedding plants that you will eat or market successfully. Plant rows north to south to provide sun to both sides of plants. Space seeds as directed and thin as advised. Pay attention to the planting zone (on-line information); and time of earliest seeding, ~~hsrdening~~hardening and transplanting. Take the seed supplier's recommendations as to depth of cover seriously. Plant tall, dense-foliage and ground vine types on the periphery of the garden plot to maximize sun to other types of plants and to permit localised additional watering. The watering demands of plant types can vary significantly – and overwatering can be as disastrous as underwatering. One timed-watering uniformly and universally applied each day may not treat some plants fairly,_- and added localised additional water may be required (e.g. blueberries, melons and pumpkins). If practical water plants with house 'grey water' effluent first, then rain collected water and then, as a last resort, municipal potable water. While gravity or pressure fed ~~drip~~drip, irrigation is complex - it is the preferred method for practically all types. Unlined ditch irrigation is not recommended since the first plants get many times the water of the last plants along the path of flow. Sprinkler irrigator bases should be elevated above the height of all plants that are to be affected – the bases should not be placed on the ground.

Do not get frustrated, get educated.

Animals

Animals are a bit more problematic, you need more space and they will need a greater or lesser amount of care. Chickens are probably the ideal livestock for the backyard pastoralist. They are cheap to acquire and feed, comparatively quiet and easy to house and they provide eggs, manure and feathers. They can be housed in a moveable coop which located over vegetable beds. They clean up bugs and weeds (after the plant cycle is completed) dig up the beds and manure them in-situ. You must, however, must make sure they can't dig there way out and get access to your growing vegetables – they are very abrasive and where you have chickens and plants together you wind up with just chickens.

A hen can lay only one egg in a day and will have some days when it does not lay an egg at all. The reasons for this laying schedule relate to the hen reproductive system. A hen's body begins forming an egg shortly after the previous egg is laid, and it takes 26 hours for an egg to form fully.

If you don't have enough room for vertebrates, maybe you could try insects (bees) or mollusks (snails). Of the two, snails are the easiest but you have to be able to consume the end product – escargot – or there is not much point. Bees do require some knowledge and equipment but give you honey, wax, by-products (e.g. Royal Jelly) and pollination in return.

Urban apiculture has undergone a renaissance in the first decade of the 21st century, and urban beekeeping is seen by many as a growing trend. Some have found that "city bees" are actually healthier than "rural bees" because there are fewer pesticides and greater biodiversity. Urban bees may fail to find forage, however, and homeowners can use their landscapes to help feed local bee populations by planting flowers that provide nectar and pollen. An environment of year-round, uninterrupted bloom creates an ideal environment for colony reproduction.

You may want to look at keeping rabbits for meat. The rabbit requires high levels of fibre in its diet for efficient gut movement and to encourage chewing to keep their continually growing teeth trim. Feeding good quality hay alongside a prepared pet food is always advised. Another good source of fibre is grass. In fact, only hay and grass can wear down teeth, so their importance in the diet cannot be underestimated. Their pelts may provide income - if value-added work is done. Animals like rabbits, sheep, goats, bees, and chickens can provide you with more than enough to meet your in-home requirement of vital foods (e.g. milk, eggs, honey, meat and materials like wool. The excesses can be marketed to provide income. Build a pond and raise fish for food. Freeze food as one preservation method (particularly if wild meat is a staple).

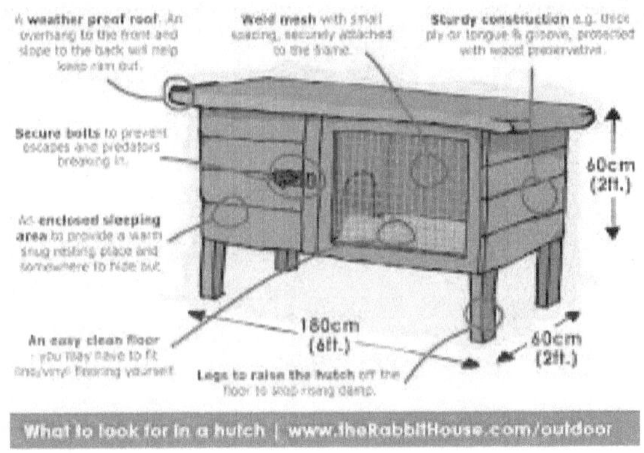

Preserve foods by dehydration. In this method, the water is slowly evaporated out of the food, without actually cooking it. There are three different methods: air-dried, sun-dried, or kiln-dried. Food from your home can easily be sun-dried with little to no ~~store bought~~store-bought equipment, whereas the air or kiln method requires purchasing some equipment. All of these can be very cost-effective ways of storing food. After drying, they are stored in evacuated airtight containers. Commercially prepared products will usually contain an oxygen absorber.

Introduce preservation with freeze dried foods. This is the method of preserving food that retains the flavour and nutritional value of fresh foods through freezing. It decreases bulk and decreases weight. Fresh or cooked foods are flash frozen and then put in large vacuum chamber that can remain as cold as -40°C. Next, a very small amount of heat is applied and the ice evaporates without ever turning back into water. This removes almost all of the moisture from the product. Then the food is canned or bagged, along with an oxygen absorber to maintain freshness, and labeled. This is good for long term storage and is easy to use at a later date because it only needs hot water to prepare it. This process produces a shelf life similar to that of dehydrated foods.

The best place to store the bulk of your long-term foods is in a basement that is kept cool and dark: 15°C or cooler. This will extend the shelf life as long as possible. The next best place would be a windowless pantry that can also be kept cool. Temperature is very important, the warmer it is, the shorter the time your food will stay edible.

Modify and use a 4-H SMALL ANIMAL HUSBANDRY SCORE CARD (for use with poultry and rabbit projects) - a ~~100 point~~ 100-point survey.

A: SHELTER AND PREMISES 20 Points - If a cage/kennel is used, is it clean, safe, of appropriate size & suitable for number of animals? - Is there adequate cover from the elements? - Does animal have regular access to exercise in a clean, safe environment? - Is maintenance of the living area conducted on a regular basis? - If applicable, are fences, shelters & cages in good repair? - Is manure managed appropriately & on a regular basis?

B: FOOD AND WATER 20 Points - Is animal fed at regular times? - Does condition of animal(s) indicate proper balance of feed? - Is food of good quality, free from mould & stored in a safe, dry place? - Are food bowls, water bottles, etc. kept clean? - Is clean, fresh water available at all times? - Are supplements/treats provided as needed?

C: CARE OF ANIMAL(~~S) 20~~S) 20 Points - Does animal receive regular grooming with adequate & clean grooming equipment? - Does the animal have toys/stimulus/nest material available to play with? - Are adequate first aid materials available, & kept in a convenient spot? - Does the member know how to use the first aid materiels with these animals - Is the animal healthy?

D: CARE OF EQUIPMENT 5 Points - Is equipment (collar, leash, show mat, showstick, etc.) in good condition, clean & stored properly? - Is the equipment the correct size for the animal? - Does the member have adequate materials for cleaning & preserving their equipment?

E: SAFETY 20 Points - Is the animal handled in such a way that both the member & the animal are safe? - Is there an appropriate area in which the animal may be confined & worked with? - Does the member have the knowledge that would show that he/she understands the need for cleanliness for the safety of the community, the member's family & the neighbours? (e.g. fly & rodent control, placement of water & food bowls, noise considerations, animals contained)

F: OPTIONS 15 Points - Member to describe safety rules that he/she follows when working with her/his animal. - Member to answer two questions regarding the practice of husbandry. Inspector to develop the questions. (e.g. grooming techniques, responsible breeding practices, health concerns, etc.)

Energy

We all use energy in our lives, to cook our food, power our vehicles, computers and TV, even to purify our water - so it is essential to have some way of harvest our own energy without relying on the 'grid' or the oil companies (well, reducing our reliance on them anyway)

Solar Capture

In a suburban or rural setting, the easiest method that is least likely to offend the neighbours is direct use of the sun's effulgence – assuming your location gets enough 'radiation', and the aspect and panel inclination permits. The sun can be used directly to cook food, heat water or dry food for preservative purposes or heat rooms. Hand fashioned solar ovens work remarkably well, and a solar food drier works well. A commercial solar water heater can save dollars in a short-time. Similarly, a reflecting parabolic solar cooker can boil, fry and stir fry as well as bake.

Adding skylights and large, energy efficient windows to take advantage of natural light. A simple water window glass framed black polyethylene pipe system can provide insolated heated water to a home.

Most equipment that makes direct use of the sun can be made cheaply
 (sometimes even out of discarded cardboard or wood and aluminium foil) by almost anyone with a few tools. This keeps the costs to s minimum.

Solar Hot-Water System

Electricity generation has more options but requires more investment and you need to know more to manage your personal energy supply. The easiest (but not cheapest) option is to buy a stack of solar photovoltaic panels and mount them on the roof or wherever. Then get an inverter (converts 12 volts direct current to 120 volts alternating current) and plug the panels into the inverter and then have an electrician wire your inverter back into the hydro grid through a meter that can run both ways.

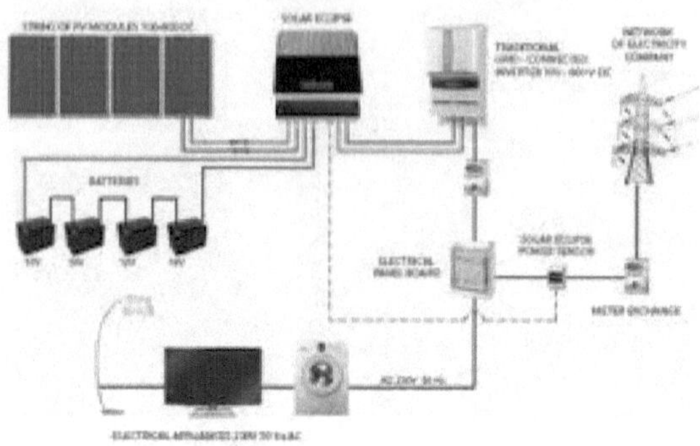

That way the power you produce goes into the grid and then you use the power back from the grid as required. This is good financially and environmentally - but if the grid goes down, you're stymied without power. Across Canada, home owners are adding solar panels to their roofs in order to save electricity and to reduce their power bills. They are choosing to use their own solar energy first, and many homes meet 20-50% of their annual power needs from their rooftop system, without changing their overall power-consumption lifestyle demands. By reducing the ~~power~~power, you use, the savings improve even more; and that is an underlying theme within self-sufficiency. The cost of installing turn-key solar power system on a mid-sized home is between $Can 30,000 to $40,000 dollars, which covers about 30 panels. If you're connecting off the grid, expect a higher price tag to cover the cost of extra wiring and materials.

Panels with Aspect of Pitched Roof Installation South and West

Typical Panel 12V to 120V Inverter

To be independent of the grid you need batteries which are heavy, expensive and do eventually require replacement. Battery technologies are advancing even as this is being written; cycling, life expectancy and weight are all improving (though not cost). You also need to know more to operate the system. It is not however rocket science as can studied on-line. Alternatively, you can run on 12 volts as well as the normal AC voltage for where you are becoming independent of the supply-chain system. Even refrigerators can be run on 12V direct current.

Consider using a diesel power generator to augment other systems of power generation at peak times - and get off the grid entirely if this is feasible (see bio-diesel discussed below).

Wind Capture

You can buy or kit-build a wind powered power source using an electricity generator (direct current) or alternator. Most home-made ones are based on a car alternator that is rectified to 12vdc. You can pay thousands of dollars for a commercial wind generator but they tend to be more quiet and unobtrusive and require less maintenance. The problem with wind generators is that they are obvious. They can upset the neighbours with noise and they may be regarded as. You may also be required to get government approval for erection. Pressurized water can also run rudimentary dc power generation (though water generally costs). Municipal water with an available house pressure of 35-psi with a flow-rate of 10-gpm will produce about 1/8-Hp (approximately 90-W after conversion power losses). Dramatically improved horsepower is achievable in settings where 'vertical heads' from reliable water sources produce more than municipal pressures.

Consider geothermal heating, hot water (and power generation). A geothermal heat pump or ground source heat pump (GSHP) is a central heating and/or cooling system that transfers heat to or from the ~~ground.It~~ground.

It uses the earth as a heat source (in the winter) or a heat sink (in the summer). This design takes advantage of the moderate temperatures in the ground to boost efficiency and reduce the operational costs of heating and cooling systems, and may be combined with solar heating to form a geosolar system with even greater efficiency. They are also known by other names, including geoexchange, earth-coupled, earth energy systems. The engineering and scientific communities prefer the terms "*geoexchange*" or "*ground source heat pumps*". Ground source heat pumps harvest heat absorbed at the Earth's surface from solar energy. The temperature in the ground below 6 metres (20 ft) is roughly equal to the mean annual air temperature at that latitude at the surface. At 44 degrees North (Toronto, Montreal, Vancouver) the mean annual air temperature is estimated to be 8 degrees C.

Depending on latitude, the temperature beneath the upper 6 metres of Earth's surface maintains a nearly constant temperature between 10 and 16 °C if the temperature is undisturbed by the presence of a heat pump. Like a refrigerator or air conditioner, these systems use a heat pump to force the transfer of heat from the ground. Heat pumps can transfer heat from a cool space to a warm space, against the natural direction of flow, or they can enhance the natural flow of heat from a warm area to a cool one. The core of the heat pump is a loop of refrigerant pumped through a vapour-compression refrigeration cycle that moves heat. Air-source heat pumps are more efficient at heating than pure electric heaters, even when extracting heat from cold winter air, although efficiencies begin dropping significantly as outside air temperatures drop below 5 °C. A ground source heat pump exchanges heat with the ground. This is much more energy-efficient because underground temperatures are more stable than air temperatures through the year. Seasonal variations drop off with depth and disappear below 7 metres to 12 ~~metres due~~metres due to thermal inertia. Like a cave, the shallow ground temperature is warmer than the air above during the winter and cooler than the air in the summer. A ground source heat pump extracts ground heat in the winter (for heating) and transfers heat back into the ground in the summer (for cooling). Some systems are designed to operate in one mode only, heating or cooling, depending on

Ground source heat pumps (GSHPs) are among the most energy efficient technologies for providing HVAC and water heating.

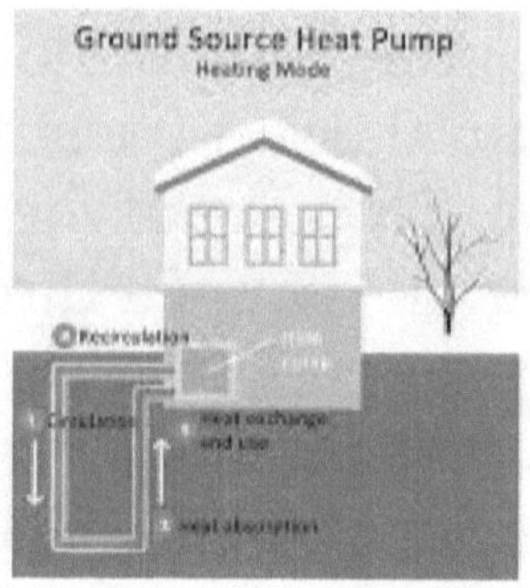

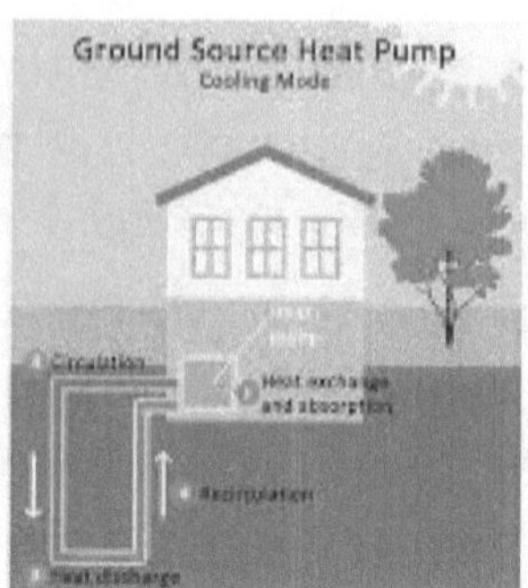

Setup costs are higher than for conventional systems, but the difference is usually returned in improved energy savings in 3 to 10 years, and even shorter lengths of time with tax credits and incentives.

Payback period for installing a ground source heat pump in a detached residence

Country	Payback period for replacing		
	natural gas	heating oil	electric heating
Canada	13 years	3 years	6 years
US	12 years	5 years	4 years
Germany	net loss	8 years	2 years

Notes:

- Highly variable with energy prices.
- Government subsidies not included.
- Climate differences not evaluated.

Geothermal heat pump systems are reasonably warranted by manufacturers, and their working life is estimated at 25 years for inside components and 50-300 years for outside components. The most recent data from an analysis of 2011-2012 showed an average cost of residential systems of about $US26,700 for a typical (4 ton) home system. One source in Canada placed prices in the range of $CAN30,000-$34,000. As of 2004, there were over one million units installed worldwide, with an annual growth rate of 10%. Capital costs may be offset by government subsidies; for example, Ontario offered $7000 for residential systems installed in the 2009 fiscal year.

Bio Diesel and Ethanol

Bio-diesel and ethanol, prepared at home, can power re-fitted vehicles. Biodiesel is a diesel fuel substitute used in diesel engines made from renewable materials such as:

- Plant oils: canola, camelina, soy, flax, jatropha, mahua, pongamia pinnata, mustard, coconut, palm, hemp and sunflower;

- Waste cooking oil: yellow or tap grease;
- Other oils: fish, and algae;
- Animal fats: beef or sheep tallow, pork lard, or poultry fat; and
- Celluosic feedstock consisting of agriculture and forest biomass.

The feedstock goes through a process called *transesterification_*and consists of fatty acid methyl esters (FAME). Transesterification is a reaction between the oil or animal fat with an alcohol and a catalyst. The chemical reaction of transesterification produces two products - glycerol and an ester called biodiesel. Raw vegetable oil or animal fats which have not undergone a chemical/refining process is not considered biodiesel and is not recommended for use in diesel engines.

Biodiesel is one common example of a renewable diesel. Hydrogenation-derived renewable diesel (HDRD) is another type of renewable diesel produced by hydrotreating of similar fat or ~~oil based~~oil-based biodiesel feedstock. Other technologies to turn biomass into renewable diesel are being developed. Currently, in Canada, regulations demand a renewable component of retailed diesel of at least 2%; with a 'view' to later stepped increases.

Ethanol distillates can be refined from yeast fermentation of a number of vegetable ingredients. Many vehicles are already marketed for flex-fuel use of ethanol blended gasolines.

Water

Water requires energy to collect, treat, store, filter and move it into your home and is remarkably cheap for all of that If you want to be self sufficient or more sustainable then it makes sense to harvest the water from your roof. Depending on your climate, size of your roof, size of your storage and needs it is possible to be run your water needs off rainwater alone. To do it successfully you may need to make some changes. Canadian average daily water use dropped by 27% from 342 litres per person in 1991 to 251 litres per person in 2011. This figure can be easily halved by simple in-home conservation measures alone.

Some automatic washing machines can chew through tens of litres of water per cycle, and toilets can use 9 litres or more of drinkable water to get rid of 100ml of human waste, which uses up reserves of collected water quickly. There are many ways to save water such as putting bath or clothes washing water on the garden and using it to flush the toilet. Introducing a low-flush toilet-toilet that uses significantly less water than a full-flush toilet is advisable. Low-flush toilets use 4.8 less per flush, as opposed to 8 litres or more (a reduction of at least 40%). Try installing at least one high-use composting toilet to thoroughly defeat water consumption in a drive to self sufficiency.

As with electricity, the more water you can store, the better -- and water tanks tend cost less (per litre stored) the bigger they are, but itits Rainwater collection barrel system in series
your conditions (e.g. providing a 'head' of water resulting in pressure, such as with flat roof capture-open store systems - rather than pumping up on ground rain-collected water).

Even a ~~200 litre~~200-litre lined or cathodically protected steel drum or a plastic 60 litre (new) garbage ~~depends~~ on

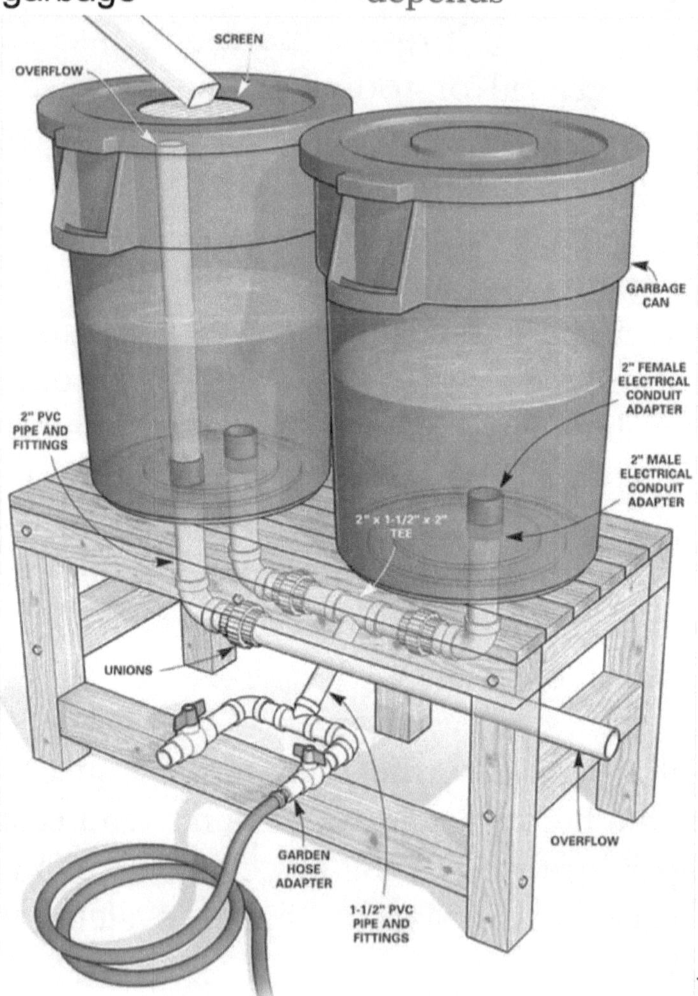

Rainwater collection barrel system in series

your conditions (e.g. providing a 'head' of water resulting in pressure, such as with flat roof capture-open store systems - rather than pumping up on ground rain-collected water). Even a 200 litre lined or cathodically protected steel drum or a plastic 60 litre (new) garbage

can will allow you to store some water - and any water storage is better than none.

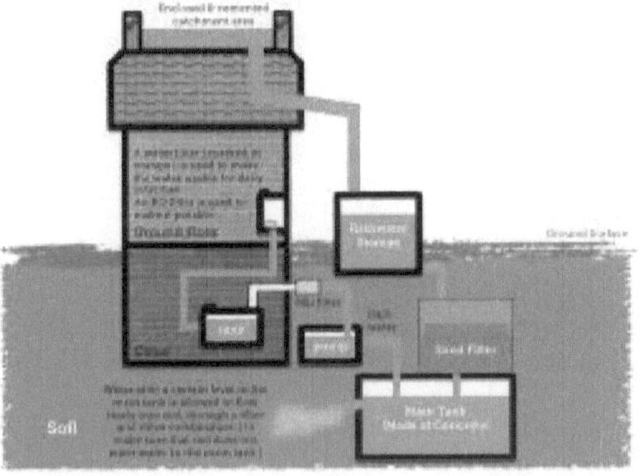

Flat Roof Capture and Store

Black poly ball evaporation inhibition systems coupled with capture store systems also provide a degree of radiant heat transfer to the rain water collected.

Sub-Urban Self-Sufficiency

Sub-Urban Self-Sufficiency

Selected Readings

1. *Maurice Grenville ~~Kains~~Kain's (1973). Five acres and independence. ISBN 0-486-20974-1.*
2. *Guilherme de Oliveira e Silva; Patrick Hendrick (September 15, 2016). "Lead-acid batteries coupled with photovoltaics for increased electricity self-sufficiency in households". Applied Energy. 178: 856. doi:10.1016/j.apenergy.2016.06.003.*
3. *~~Vanini~~Venini, Phillip (2014). Off the Grid: Re-Assembling Domestic Life. p. 10.*
4. *Adey, Peter (2014). The Routledge Handbook of Mobilities. p. 117.*
5. *Stanley, John (November 1, 2007). "Survival guide aimed at complacent urbanites". The Arizona Republic. Retrieved 2012-08-07.*
6. *Lundin, Cody. "About Cody Lundin". Retrieved 2012-08-07.*
7. *Rosen, Nick. Off the Grid: Inside the Movement for More Space, Less Government, and True Independence. Penguin. ISBN 0143117386.*
8. *"Off-Grid Communities". Aboriginal Affairs and Northern Development Canada. 2012-05-01.*

9. *"IEA PV Roadmap" (PDF).*

10. *"Photovoltaic off-grid map". Infinergia Consulting. Retrieved 2012-04-1*

11. *Maslow, A.H. (1943). "A theory of human motivation". Psychological Review. 50 (4): 370–96. doi:10.1037/h0054346 – via psychclassics.yorku.ca.*

12. *Maslow, A (1954). Motivation and personality. New York, NY: Harper. ISBN 0-06-041987-3.*

13. *Mittelman, W. (1991). "Maslow's study of self-actualization: A reinterpretation". Journal of Humanistic Psychology. 31 (1): 114–135. doi:10.1177/0022167891311010.*

14. *Goble, F. (1970). The third force: The psychology of Abraham Maslow.* Richmond, CA: Maurice Bassett Publishing. pp. 62.

15. *Villarica, H. (August 17, 2011). "Maslow 2.0: A new and improved recipe for happiness". theatlantic.com.*

16. *Tay, L.; Diener, E. (2011). "Needs and subjective well-being around the world". Journal of Personality and Social Psychology. 101 (2): 354–365. doi:10.1037/a0023779.*

17. *Bugental DB (2000). "Acquisition of the Algorithms of Social Life: A Domain-*

Based Approach". *Psychological Bulletin*. 126 (2): 178–219. doi:10.1037/0033-2909.126.2.187. PMID 10748640.

18. Wahba, M. A.; Bridwell, L. G. (1976). "Maslow reconsidered: A review of research on the need hierarchy theory". *Organizational Behavior and Human Performance*. 15 (2): 212–240. doi:10.1016/0030-5073(76)90038-6.

19. Cianci, R.; Gambrel, P. A. (2003). "Maslow's hierarchy of needs: Does it apply in a collectivist culture". *Journal of Applied Management and Entrepreneurship*. 8 (2): 143–161.

20. Kenrick, D. (May 19, 2010). "Rebuilding Maslow's pyramid on an evolutionary foundation". psychologytoday.com/.

21. Kenrick, D. T.; Griskevicius, V.; Neuberg, S. L.; Schaller, M. (2010). "Renovating the pyramid of needs: Contemporary extensions built upon ancient foundations". *Perspectives on Psychological Science*. 5: 292. doi:10.1177/1745691610369469.

22. Tang, T. L.; West, W. B. (1997). "The importance of human needs during peacetime, retrospective peacetime, and the Persian Gulf War".

International Journal of Stress Management. 4 (1): 47–62.

23. Goebel, B. L.; Brown, D. R. (1981). "Age differences in motivation related to Maslow's need hierarchy". *Developmental Psychology. 17: 809–815.* doi:10.1037/0012-1649.17.6.809.

24. Clutton-Brock, Juliet (1999). *A Natural History of Domesticated Mammals. Cambridge University Press.* pp. 1–2. ISBN 978-0-521-63495-3.

25. "History of the domestication of animals". *Historyworld.* Retrieved 3 June 2017.

26. Webster, John (2013). *Animal Husbandry Regained: The Place of Farm Animals in Sustainable Agriculture. Routledge.* pp. 4–10. ISBN 978-1-84971-420-4.

27. Blench, Roger (17 May 2001). 'You can't go home again' – Pastoralism in the new millennium (PDF). *London, UK: Overseas Development Institute.* p. 12.

28. Blount, W.P. (2013). *Intensive Livestock Farming. Elsevier.* pp. 360–62. ISBN 978-1-4831-9565-0.

29. Dryden, Gordon McL. (2008). *Animal Nutrition Science. CABI..* ISBN 978-1-78064-056-3.

30. Dryden, Gordon McL. (2008). *Animal Nutrition Science*. CABI. pp. 16–19. ISBN 978-1-84593-412-5.

31. "What farm animals eat". Food Standards Agency. Retrieved 18 May 2017.

32. Turner, Jacky (2010). *Animal Breeding, Welfare and Society*. Routledge. p. Introduction. ISBN 978-1-136-54187-2.

33. Jarman, M.R.; Clark, Grahame; Grigson, Caroline; Uerpmann, H.P.; Ryder, M.L. (1976). "Early Animal Husbandry". *The Royal Society*. 275 (936): 85–97. doi:10.1098/rstb.1976.0072.

34. Fraser, Douglas (14 February 2017). "Scottish salmon farming's sea lice 'crisis'". BBC. Retrieved 20 May 2017.

35. "Parasite control". Animal Health Ireland. Retrieved 20 May 2017.

36. Norrgren, Leif; Levengood, Jeffrey M. (2012). *Ecology and Animal Health*. Baltic University Press. pp. 103–04. ISBN 978-91-86189-12-9.

37. W.; Ademosun, A. A.; von Kaufmann, R.; Hoste, C.; Rains, A. Blair. "5. Livestock resources and management". Food and Agriculture Organization. Retrieved 24 May 2017.

38. *"Livestock Species". Texas A&M University Department of Agriculture and Life Sciences. Retrieved 24 May 2017.*

39. *Steinfeld, H.; Mäki-Hokkonen, J. "A classification of livestock production systems". Food and Agriculture Organization. Retrieved 24 May 2017.*

40. *Godinho, Denise. "Animal Husbandry in Organic Agriculture". Food and Agriculture Organization. Retrieved 25 May 2017.*

41.*Gregory, Neville G.; Grandin, Temple (2007). Animal Welfare and Meat Production. CABI. pp. 1–2. ISBN 978-1-84593-216-9.*

42. *"About egg laying hens". Compassion in World Farming. Retrieved 26 May 2017.*

43. *"Growing meat chickens". Australian Chicken Meat Federation Inc. 2013. Retrieved 26 May 2017.*

44. Sherwin, C.M., (2010). Turkeys: Behavior, Management and Well-Being. In "The Encyclopaedia of Animal Science". Wilson G. Pond and Alan W. Bell (Eds). Marcel Dekker. pp. 847–49

45. *"Global Aquaculture Production". Fishery Statistical Collections. Food and Agriculture Organization of the United Nations. Retrieved 26 May 2017.*

46. *Mosig, John; Fallu, Ric (2004). Australian Fish Farmer: A Practical Guide to Aquaculture. Landlinks Press. pp. 25–28. ISBN 978-0-643-06865-0.*

47. *"Fixed combs". Bees for Development. Archived from the original on 18 May 2011. Retrieved 22 May 2017.*

48. *Jabr, Ferris (1 September 2013). "The Mind-Boggling Math of Migratory Beekeeping". Scientific American. Retrieved 22 May 2017.*

49. *"Livestock a major threat to environment". Food and Agriculture Organizations of the United Nations.*

50. *Whitford, Walter G. (2002). Ecology of desert systems. Academic Press. p. 277. ISBN 978-0-12-747261-4.*

51. *"Unit 9: Biodiversity Decline // Section 7: Habitat Loss: Causes and Consequences". Annenberg Learner..*

52. *Monteny, Gert-Jan; Andre Bannink; David Chadwick (2006). "Greenhouse Gas Abatement Strategies for Animal Husbandry, Agriculture, Ecosystems, and Environment". Agriculture, Ecosystems, and Environment. 112 (2–3): 163–170. doi:10.1016/j.agee.2005.08.015. Retrieved 5 June 2013.*

53.　　Hewson, C.J. (2003). "What is animal welfare? Common definitions and their practical consequences". *The Canadian Veterinary Journal*. 44 (6): 496–99. PMC 340178. PMID 12839246.

54.　　Broom, D.M. (1991). "Animal welfare: concepts and measurement". *Journal of Animal Science*. 69 (10): 4167–75. PMID 1778832.

55.　　Garner, R. (2005). *Animal Ethics*. Polity Press.

56.　　Rafferty, Kevin (April 1997). "An Information Survival Kit for the Prospective Residential Geothermal Heat Pump Owner" (PDF). *Geo-Heat Centre Quarterly Bulletin*. 18 (2). Klamath Falls, Oregon: Oregon Institute of Technology. ISSN 0276-1084.

57.　　"Geothermal Technologies Program: Geothermal Basics". *US Department of Energy*. Archived from the original on 2008-10-04. Retrieved 2011-03-30.

58.　　Dowlatabadi, H (9 November 2007). "Strategic GHG reduction through the use of ground source heat pump technology" (PDF). *Environmental Research Letters*. 2. UK: IOP Publishing. pp. 044001 8pp.

Bibcode:2007ERL.....2d4001H.
doi:10.1088/1748-9326/2/4/044001.
ISSN 1748-9326. Retrieved 2009-03-22.

59. Tomislav Kurevija, Domagoj Vulin, Vedrana Krapec. "Influence of Undisturbed Ground Temperature and Geothermal Gradient on the Sizing of Borehole Heat Exchangers" page 1262 ~~Faculty of Mining, Geology and Petroleum Engineering, University of Zagreb,May~~Zagreb, May 2011. Accessed: October 2013.

60. *"Energy Savers: Geothermal Heat Pumps". Energysavers.gov. Retrieved 2011-03-30.*

61. *"Geothermal Technologies Program: Tennessee Energy Efficient Schools Initiative Ground Source Heat Pumps". Apps1.eere.energy.gov. 2010-03-29. Archived from the original on 2010-05-28. Retrieved 2011-03-30.*

62. *Lund, J.; Sanner, B.; Rybach, L.; Curtis, R.; Hellström, G. (September 2004). "Geothermal (Ground Source) Heat Pumps, A World Overview" (PDF). Geo-Heat Centre Quarterly Bulletin. 25 (3). Klmath Falls, Oregon: Oregon Institute of Technology. pp. 1–10. ISSN 0276-1084. Retrieved 2009-03-21.*

63. *"Environmental Technology Verification Report" (PDF). U.S.*

Environmental Protection Agency. Archived from the original (PDF) on 2008-02-27. Retrieved December 3, 2015.

64. *"Ground Source Heat Pumps (Earth Energy Systems)". Heating and Cooling with a Heat Pump. Natural Resources Canada, Office of Energy Efficiency. Archived from the original on 2009-04-03. Retrieved 2009-03-24..*

65. *Chiasson, A.D. (1999). "Advances in modeling of ground source heat pump systems" (PDF). Oklahoma State University. Retrieved 2009-04-23.*

66. *Rezaei, B.; Amir, Kolahdouz; Dargush, G. F.; Weber, A. S. (2012a). "Ground source heat pump pipe performance with Tire Derived Aggregate". International Journal of Heat and Mass Transfer. 55 (11-12): 2844–2853. doi:10.1016/j.ijheatmasstransfer.2012.02.004.*

67. *"Geothermal Ground Loops". Informed Building. Retrieved 2009-06-08.*

68. *Orio, Carl D.; Johnson, Carl N.; Rees, Simon J.; Chiasson, A.; Deng, Zheng; Spitler, Jeffrey D. (2004). "A Survey of Standing Column Well Installations in North America" (PDF).*

ASHRAE Transactions. 11 (4). ASHRAE. pp. 637–655. Archived from the original (PDF) on 2010-06-26. Retrieved 2009-03-25.

69.   Geothermal Heat Pumps. National Renewable Energy Laboratory.

70.   *"AHRI Directory of water-to-air geothermal heat pumps".*

71. *"Energy Star Program Requirements for Geothermal Heat PUmps" (PDF). Partner Commitments. Energy Star. Retrieved 2009-03-24.*

72.   *"annex 9". National Inventory Report 1990–* 2006:Greenhouse *2006: Greenhouse Gas Sources and Sinks in Canada. Government of Canada. May 2008.   ISBN 978-1-100-11176-6. ISSN 1706-3353.*

○

73.   Glaser, Bruno, Johannes Lehmann, and Wolfgang Zech, *Ameliorating physical and chemical properties of highly weathered soils in the tropics with charcoal – a review,* Biology and Fertility of Soils 35.4 219-220 (2002)

74.   *"Australian Society of Horticultural Science – Australian Society of Horticultural Science".*

75.   *"Home – NJHA".*

76.   *"RNZIH – Royal New Zealand Institute of Horticulture – Home Page".*
77. *"The Global Horticulture Initiative"*

About the Author

Mark Roberts-Seymour, B.A.Sc., P.Eng., CD, ACG, OFS is a Canadian Professional Forensic Engineer, a recognised stoneworks conservator, Chartered Demographer, non-fiction author, lay-brother, professional public speaker (Toastmaster Advanced Communicator Gold), technical paper referee, statistical assessor, and editor.

Over succeeding years his publications have included:

- Christian Transmigration
- Old, Unemployed and Pissed: Late Career Canadians Coping with Long-term Unemployment
- Restructuring a Broken Canadian Economic-Democracy
- Three Proto-Christian Orthodoxies, The Gospel of Paul, Alexandrian Orthodoxy and Proto-Christian Gnosticism: A Comparison

Sub-Urban Self-Sufficiency

- <u>Clinical Happiness: Measurement, Measures, Goals and Habit Conditioning</u>
- <u>Anglicanism: From Henry to Henrietta</u>
- <u>Cyborg: Smartphone Reliance, AI and Transhumanism</u>
- <u>An Afterlife: Who Cares! Quotations on an After-life with Biographical notes</u>
- <u>Conservation of Heritage Cemeteries,</u>
- <u>Green Revolutions – Will they be Enough,</u>
- <u>Suburban and Ex-Urban Self Sufficiency,</u>
- <u>Life Extension for Seniors Book 1: Expectations, Ageing Inhibition, Nutrition, Brain 'Wiring', Habits, Exercise and Ethics</u>
- <u>The Working Poor: Who are Poor and What Can Be Done: A Central British Columbia Case Study</u>
- <u>Life Extension for Seniors Book 2: Methods, Research, Supplementation, Health and Life-Prolonging Strategies</u>
- <u>Abrahamic Gnosticism is not Scary,</u>
- <u>Proofs of God – Philosophy of Religion and Science Converge,</u>
- <u>Anglicanism – From Henry to Henrietta,</u>

<u>Sub-Urban Self-Sufficiency</u>

- Happiness: Biochemistry, Goals and Habituation,
- The Parable of the Prodigal Son - Death, Rebirth, Recognition and Reconciliation,
- Nutrition for Older Workers,
- Nutrient Supplements for the Older Worker,
- Canadian Systems: Changing our Economic-Democracy,
- Gnosticism as Revelation: from St. Paul to C.G. Jung,
- Sabotage, Wealth and New Classes,
- Christian Metempsychosis: Elijah and John the Baptist,
- Sanctification – It's for Everyone!
- The Gospel of Paul, Christian Gnosticism and Alexandrian Orthodoxy – A Comparison,
- An Afterlife, Who Cares! *Quotations from 231 sources*
- Renovating the Canadian Economic-Democratic System,
- To Coin a Phrase or Not to Coin a Phrase: Clichés, Metaphors and Euphemisms in Use,

Sub-Urban Self-Sufficiency

- Canadian Systems: Changing our Economic-Democracy,
- It Can't Happen Here: Future Mechanisation, Despair and Suicide

To access further information on these books [or for purchase], links to the Distributor Amazon.com are indicated in the list preceding.

Mark acted for more thirty years as a Registered Professional Engineer (P.Eng., PE, ing.), technical author and editor for: The Government of BC (Lands Forests and Water Resources), BH Levelton and Associates, Warnock Hersey Professional Services, Heritage Technologies Press, RM Hardy and Associates, G.W. Spratt Limited and others. Mark also owned and managed a private Materials Engineering firm for an additional ten years (Roberts Seymour and Associates Limited).

He remains active in several service, political and social justice organisations as well as maintaining his professional standings. He is married, the father of four adult children and many grandchildren, and calls Vernon, British Columbia, Canada his home. Mark Roberts-

Seymour can be reached directly by email at merscanada@gmail.com and by telephone at (250) 306-0550. For keynote speaking and seminar leadership contact (250) 721-5683.